Step-by-Step Mexican Cuisine

Step-by-Step

Mexican Cuisine

Pankaj Misra

AMAN PUBLICATIONS
NEW DELHI

Published by
Rajiv Jain for **Aman Publications**
LG-4A, Ganpati Bhawan,
4675-B/21, Ansari Road,
Darya Ganj, Delhi-110002
E-mail: sshjbs@yahoo.com

[The responsibility for the facts stated, conclusions reached etc. is entirely that of the Author. The publisher is not responsible for them, whatsoever.]

2026
ISBN–978-81-8204-098-4

Sole Distributor
JINDAL BOOK SERVICES
LG-4A, Ganpati Bhawan,
4675-B/21, Ansari Road,
Darya Ganj, Delhi - 110002

Cover Design & Typeset by:
Advance Publishing Concept
New Delhi

Printed by:
Balaji Offest, Delhi, India

With reverence to the medium of
my worldly manifestation and the foundation
of my value system,
My Beloved Father
Whose benign presence is earnestly remembered by me
in all my endeavors

Lt. Dr. Ram Phal Misra

And my torrent of inspiration and encouragement
My Gracious mother

Mrs. Shanti Devi Mishra

Preface

Mexican cuisine is a style of food that originates in Mexico. It is known for its varied flavors, colourful decoration, and variety of spices and ingredients, many of which are native to the country.

Basic elements

The basis of the diet is still corn and beans with chili pepper as a seasoning as they are complimentary foods. However, European contributions include pork, chicken, beef, cheese, various herbs and spices and some fruits.

The basic starch is corn in the country. While it is eaten fresh, most corn is dried, treated with lime and ground into dough. However, the most common way to eat corn in Mexico is in the form of a tortilla, which accompanies almost every dish in Mexico. Tortillas are made of corn in most of the countries.

The Mexico is known as country of chillies where thousand varieties of chillies are grown throughout the country. The most common variety is jalapenos, (also common in Mexican cuisine).

The main meats found in Mexico are pork, chicken, beef, goat and sheep. Native seafood remains popular especially along the coasts.

The most frequently used herbs and spices in Mexican cuisine are chilli powder, oregano, cilantro, epazote and cinnamon.

Cheese making in Mexico has evolved its own specialties. It is an important economic activity, especially in the north, and frequently done at home. Goat cheese is still made but it is not as popular and harder to find in stores.

Many Mexican dishes also contain lot of garlic, coriander leaves and onions.

Honey is an important ingredient in many Mexican dishes.

Rice is the most common grain in Mexican cuisine.

Ingredients used in Mexican Cuisine

Vegetables

Onions and Garlic

Onions and Garlic is the most common flavors find in Mexican food. Garlic comes fresh or in powdered form and is used in many recipes and onion which usually comes fresh or powdered. It is commonly used in conjunction with garlic.

Fresh tomatoes are used raw in salsas, and are also used as toppings. Tomatoes are not usually used to make a sauce. Cooked or canned tomatoes are also used as flavors for salads, soups and rice.

Spices

Other common flavors are oregano, cumin and chili powder. Mexican oregano gives their dishes a rich earthy flavor.

Cumin

Cumin has been around since the beginning of history. It has a toasty yet somewhat bitter taste and gives Mexican dishes a certain flavor.

Cinnamon and cloves are also used to add unique dimensions of flavor to Mexican dishes.

Beans

Another widely used ingredient is beans, such as black beans and pinto beans. They are used to make dishes such as refried beans, bean salads, soups and more.

Fats

Vegetable oil is used for cooking.

The most common cooking methods of Mexico are roasting, frying, grilling and boiling.

Contents

Fresh Tomato Salsa

Basic Mexican preparation and serve as accompaniment with any Mexican preparation.

Ingredients	Quantity
Tomatoes	300 gm
Onion	80 gm
Green chillies	04 nos
Garlic, chopped	10 gm
Coriander leaves, fine chopped	10 gm
Jalapenos peppers, chopped	20 gm
Tabasco sauce	5 ml
Lemon juice	50 ml
Salt	To Taste
White pepper	A pinch
Tomato juice	100 ml

Note: This sauce does not require cooking.

Method

- Wash tomatoes and green chillies,
- Roughly chop all the ingredients and put in to food processor to get the even and grainy texture.
- Add fine chopped onion, jalapenos garlic and mix well.
- Add tomato juice, salt, white pepper, Tabasco sauce and lemon juice.
- Add finely chopped green coriander leaves and served chill.

Roasted Tomato Salsa

Ingredients	Quantity
Tomatoes	400 gm
Olive oils	25 ml
Whole red chilli	03 nos
Green chillies	06 nos
Garlic, chopped	10 gm
Coriander leaves, fine chopped	15 gm
Jalapenos peppers, chopped	50 gm
Tabasco sauce	10 ml
Lemon juice	50 ml
Salt	To Taste
White pepper	a pinch
Tomato juice	100 ml

Method

- Wash the tomatoes, apply small cuts on tomatoes, apply olive oil one each tomatoes.
- Pre heat the oven at 200°C, put the tomatoes on greased tray and keep it in the oven for at least 10-15 minutes along with green chillies and half of the quantity of garlic.
- Remove from the oven and allow to cool.
- Remove the skin of the tomatoes.
- Cut the roasted tomatoes into quarter, deseed the tomatoes and cut them into small dices.
- Reserve the tomato juice for salsa.
- Dice jalapeno and coriander leaves
- Combine all the ingredients together and correct the seasoning and serve chill.

Roasted Garlic Salsa

Ingredients	Quantity
Tomatoes	220 gm
Garlic head	100 gm
Onion , fine chopped	50 gm
Jalapenos peppers, chopped	30 gm
Olive oil	45 ml
Tabasco sauce	10 ml
Lemon juice	10 ml
Salt	To Taste
Tomato juice	100 ml

METHOD

- ❖ Wash, peel and finely chopped onion.
- ❖ Peel of the skin of garlic, wash the tomatoes, and apply small cuts on tomatoes.
- ❖ Pre heat the oven at 200°C, put the garlic and tomatoes on greased tray and keep it in the oven for at least 20-30 minutes or until softened.
- ❖ Remove from the oven and allow to cool.
- ❖ Remove the skin of the tomatoes.
- ❖ Cut the roasted tomatoes into quarter, deseed the tomatoes and cut them into small pieces.
- ❖ Combine all the ingredients together except lime juice, put it in blender, make smooth paste and check the seasoning, add lemon juice. Serve chilled.

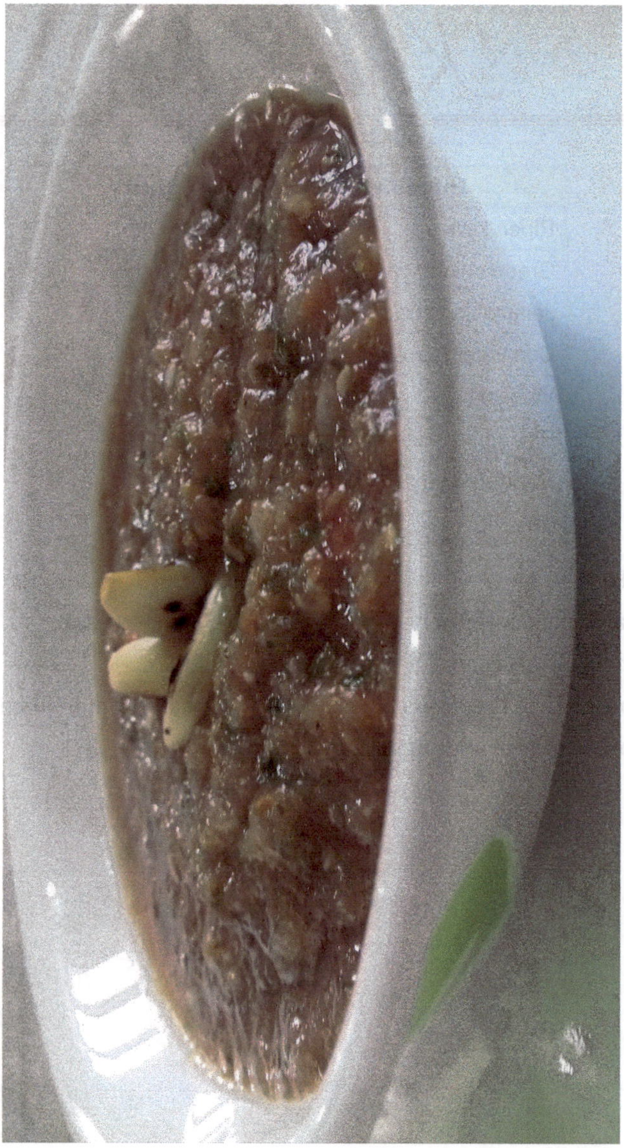

Kiwi Salsa

Ingredients	Quantity
Ripen kiwi	120 gm
Green onion , fine chopped	50 gm
Jalapenos peppers, chopped	10 gm
Coriander leaves	5 gm
Vinegar	15 ml
Pineapple juice	10 ml
Powdered sugar	5 gm
Salt	To Taste

Method

- Wash, peel and finely chopped ripen kiwi and onion.
- Finely chop coriander leaves and jalapenos.
- Combine all the ingredients together and add lemon juice.
- Chilled before serving.

Fruity Salsa

The fruity salsa is excellent with grilled chicken.

Ingredients	Quantity
Ripe mangoes	100 gm
Plum	100 gm
Tinned Pineapple slices	100 gm
Kiwi	100 gm
Crushed red chili flakes	2 gm
Lemon juice	10 ml
Powdered sugar	5 gm
Salt	To Taste
Coriander leaves	5 gm

Method

- ❖ Wash, peel, deseed to all stone fruits and cut all fruits in small dices
- ❖ Finely chop coriander leaves.
- ❖ Combine all the ingredients together and add lemon juice. Chilled before serving.

Avocado and Tomato Salsa

Ingredients	Quantity
Tomatoes	240 gm
Avocado	80 gm
Onion ,fine chopped	20 gm
Jalapenos peppers, chopped	15 gm
Coriander leaves, fine chopped	15 gm
Garlic, minced	2 nos.
Lemon juice	50 ml
Salt	To Taste

Method

- Wash the tomatoes and roughly chop them.
- Wash, peel and roughly cut to avocado and onion.
- Wash and finely chop coriander leaves.
- Combine all the ingredients together, put it in blender, make smooth paste and check the seasoning, add lemon juice. Serve chilled.

Green Mango Salsa

Ingredients	Quantity
Green Mango	250 gm
Onion, chopped	50 gm
Garlic	3 cloves
Cilantro leaves	10 gm
Jalapeno peppers, chopped	2 small
Salt	to Taste
White pepper	2 gm
Ground cumin	3 gm
Extra virgin olive oil	30 ml
Water	20 ml.

Preparation

- Peel green mangoes cut it into quarters and remove seeds.
- In a blender or food processor, place jalapenos, onion, garlic, cilantro, jalapeno peppers, salt, pepper, oregano, cumin, 2 tablespoons olive oil, and water: process until slightly chunky.

Method

- In medium saucepan over medium heat, heat remaining olive oil.
- Add the pieces of green mango and simmer for 10 to 12 minutes, stirring frequently, until slightly thickened.
- Remove from heat and pour into serving bowl.
- Cover and let stand 1-2 hours to blend flavors. Serve warm or cold.

Ripe Mango Salsa

Ingredients	Quantity
Diced Mangoes	4 nos.
Chopped red onion	15 gm
Fresh cilantro leaves, chopped	10 gm
Jalapeño, seeded and minced	01 no
Lime, juiced	10 ml
salt;	to taste

PREPARATION:

- ❖ In a serving bowl, combine the prepared mango, bell pepper, onion, cilantro and jalapeño.
- ❖ Drizzle with the juice of one lime and mix well.
- ❖ Season to taste with salt. Let the salsa rest for 10 minutes or longer to get the best flavor.

Arabiata Sauce

Ingredients	Quantity
Blanched Tomatoes	250 gm
Tomato puree	50gm
Onion diced	15 ml
Refined oil	15 ml
Green chillies	4 gm
Garlic, chopped	4 gm
Red chilli flakes	3 gm
Coriander leaves, fine chopped	15 gm
Salt	To taste
Water	50 ml
Parsley	3 gm
Black pepper powder	a pinch

Method

- Heat oil in a large skillet or saucepan over medium heat.
- Saut onion and garlic in oil for few minutes.
- Stir in wine, sugar, basil, red pepper, tomato paste, lemon juice, Italian seasoning, black pepper and tomatoes; bring to a boil. Reduce heat to medium, and simmer uncovered about 15 minutes.
- Add red chilli flakes and oregano on the top.

Rancharo Sauce

A delicious and versatile sauce perfect to top enchiladas and other dishes in the Mexican cuisine.

Ingredients	Quantity
Tomatoes diced	250 gm
Chopped onion	60 gm
Garlic, chopped	25 gm
Cooking oil	30 ml
Jalapeno chilli, seeded and diced	3 nos
Oregano	2 gm
Red chilli flake	2 gm
Salt	to taste

Cooking Method

- Heating the oil, and sauté the garlic, jalapeno and onions for 2-3 minutes.
- Reduce the heat and add in the tomatoes.
- Cook the tomatoes for about 5 or 6 minutes until they become wilted.
- Add in the seasonings and simmer for about 5 more minutes.
- Add salt and pepper and correct the seasoning.

Red Kidney Beans

This is a side dish and generally served with the main courses in Mexican dishes.

Ingredients	Quantity
Tomato puree	100 gm
Water	200 ml.
Chilli powder	3 gm
Tomatoes	150 gm
Kidney beans	100 gm
Garlic powder	3 gm
Cumin powder	3 gm
Salt	To Taste
Sugar	3 gm
Black pepper powder	4 gm
Refined oil	150 ml

Preparation

- Clean, wash and soak kidney beans for at least 6 to 8 hours.

Cooking Method

- Wash and soak kidney beans for at least 6 hour
- Refresh with fresh water and cook it with salted water and cook till it become tender enough.
- Add all the ingredients in a stock pot and simmer for 30 minutes on moderate temperature.
- Remove from flame, allow to cool and then transfer to a suitable pan.

Cilantro Dip

Ingredients	Quantity
Cilantro, finely chopped	30 gm
Sour cream	220 ml
Green onions, minced	30 gm
Green chillies	03 nos
Lime juice	15 no
Freshly ground black pepper	A pinch
Salt	To taste

Preparation

- Peel onion and chopped finely.
- Wash coriander leaves and chopped finely.
- Take sour cream and mix all ingredients together and refrigerate for at least 30 minutes.
- Serve with tortillas or as a quesadilla topping.

Sour Cream

Ingredients	Quantity
Hang curd	120 gm
Fresh cream 1 cup	350 m
Lemon juice 2 tablespoons	90 ml
Salt	to taste

Method

- Take a piece of 12″x12″ muslin cloth and put approximately 200 ml curd on it and hold at least for one hour.
- Beat the cream until thick.
- Take a fresh bowl, add the hang curd and cream well. Add the beaten curd, lemon juice and salt. Mix well and serve.

Peri Peri Sauce

A very hot sauce made with red chilli peppers.

Ingredients	Quantity
Whole red chillies	10-15 nos
Garlic	10-12 no
Red chilli flakes	A pinch
Lemon juice	20 ml
Olive oil	30 ml
Salt	to taste

Preparation

- ❖ Remove stem from red chillies and rinse with running water.
- ❖ Peel garlic and roughly chop.
- ❖ Wash and roughly chop coriander leaves
- ❖ Add all ingredients in a food processor to get smooth paste.
- ❖ Add salt and lemon juice, mix well and serve with tortilla's and other dishes.

Flour Tortilla

Ingredients	Quantity
Refined flour	100 gm
Wheat flour	20 gm
Salt	2 gm
Milk	30 ml
Water	30 ml
Egg	5 gm
Oil	3 ml
Baking powder	a pinch

Cooking Method

- Mix all the ingredients in a bowl expect milk, water & oil.
- Add milk and water slowly to make smooth and soft dough.
- Add oil at the last.
- Prepare soft dough and divide it into small ball weighing 20 g for 6″ diameter, 50 gm for 8″ diameter and 70 gm for 11″ diameter).
- Roll each ball into the required size
- Bake it over the flat top until it is half done.
- Dab the tortilla with a fork to make small holes all over.
- Wrap it in silver foil. (These tortilla may use immediately or they may store for 2-3 days under proper refrigeration).

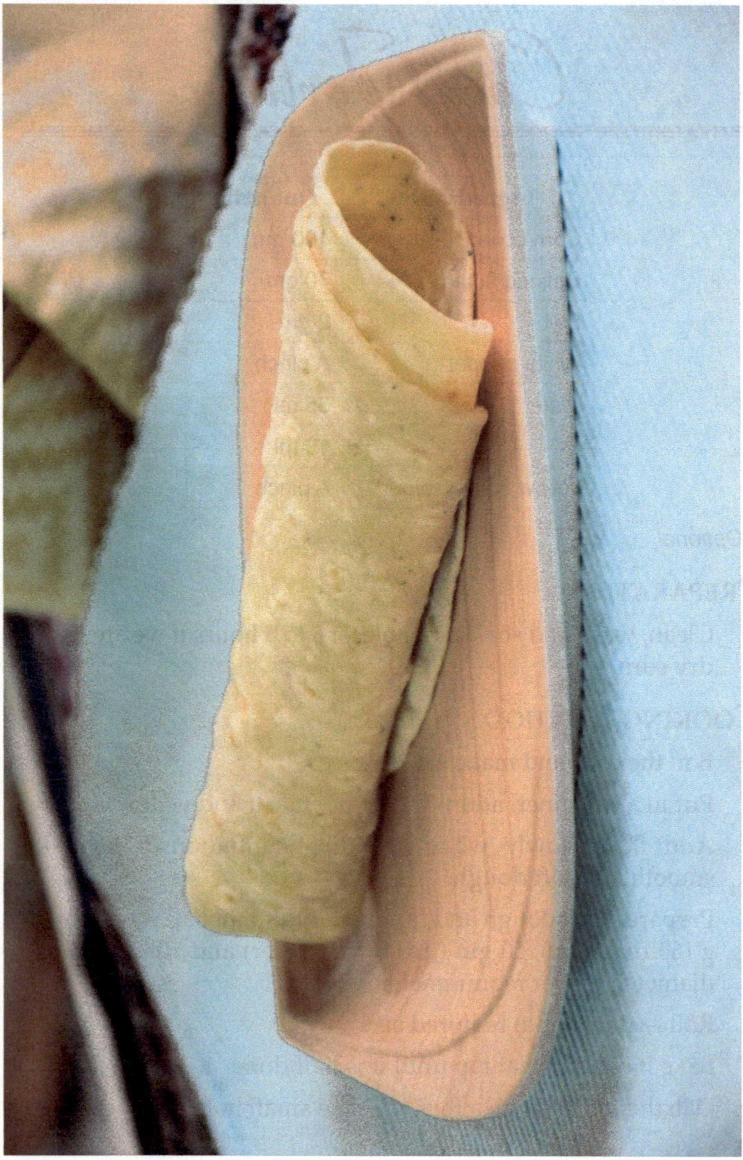

Corn Tortilla

Ingredients	Quantity
Corn boiled	100 gm
Refined flour	70 gm
Salt	2 gm
White pepper	A pinch
Water	35 ml
Oil	10 ml
Yellow edible colour *	A pinch

** Optional*

Preparation

- ❖ Clean, wash and soak corn at least 6 to 8 hours if we are using dry corn.

Cooking Method

- ❖ Boil the corn and make a paste.
- ❖ Put in a container, add white pepper, salt and yellow colour.
- ❖ Add flour slowly while kneading continuously to make smooth and soft dough.
- ❖ Prepare a soft dough and divide it into small ball weighing 20 g (6″ diameter), 50 gm (for 8″ diameter) and 70 gm for 11″ diameter) as per requirements.
- ❖ Roll each ball into required size
- ❖ Bake it over the flat top until it is half done.
- ❖ Dab the tortilla with a fork to make small holes all over.

- ❖ Take a frying pan and add refined oil heat well and when the temperature reach at smoke point*, add few pieces of tortillas.
- ❖ Fry till get light golden brown colour.

Note: *Wrap it in silver foil. (These tortilla may use immediately or they may store for 2-3 days under proper refrigeration).*

Olive & Herb Tortilla

Ingredients	Quantity
Corn boiled	90 gm
Refined flour	70 gm
Green olive	5 gm
Oregano	A pinch
Thyme	A pinch
Salt	2 gm
White pepper	A pinch
Water	35 ml
Oil	10 ml
Yellow edible colour *	A pinch

** Optional*

Preparation

- Clean, wash and soak corn at least 6 to 8 hours if we are using dry corn.

Cooking Method

- Boil the corn and make a paste along with green olives.
- Put in a container; add white pepper, salt, oregano, thyme and yellow colour.
- Add flour slowly while kneading continuously to make smooth and soft dough.
- Prepare soft dough and divide it into 70 gm and thin roll in 11″ diameter.
- Bake it over the flat top until it is half done.

- Dab the tortilla with a fork to make small holes all over.
- With the help of round cutter of 2 inch diameter and keep a side.
- Take a frying pan and add refined oil heat well fry the tortillas till get light golden brown colour.
- Remove from oil; allow to come at room temperature and its ready for use or store in air tight container for future use.

Corn Taco

Ingredients	Quantity
Corn tortilla 4”	4 nos
Refined oil – for frying	

Cooking Method

- Take a frying pan and add refined oil.
- Heat well and when the temperature reach at smoke point*, put one tortilla at a time and as soon as leave tortilla in hot oil, immediately fold with the help of tong to give semi spare shape.
- When doing so, care must be taken that there must be cavity for stuffing.
- Fry till get light golden brown colour.
- Remove from the oil. Allow to cool and bring at room temperature and use as per requirement.

* *The temperature at which oil starts to bum and generate smoke. This stage is ideal for deep frying.*

Taco Seasoning

It is made in a liquid or a powdered form both, but the powder is the most common. Basically,it is use in taco reci pes to get a spicy,rich flavor for the meats and other preparations.

Ingredients	Quantity
Red Chili Powder	10 gm
Garlic Powder	3 gm
Onion powder	2 gm
Red Pepper Flakes (Aleppo peppers)	4 gm
Oregano	4 gm
Paprika	5 gm
Roasted Cumin Powder	5 gm
Salt	15 gm
White Pepper	10

Preparation

- Combine all ingredients in a bowl.
- Make fine powder of it. And store in a tightly closed container.

Onion Straws

The onion straws serve as an accompaniment in Mexican cuisine.

Ingredients	Quantity
Butter milk	300 ml
Onion rings (2mm thick)	75 gm
Refined flour	75 gm
Salt	100 gm
Pepper powder	to taste
Oregano	1 gm
Basil	1 gm
Sugar	3gm
Cayenne pepper	2 gm
Refined oil (for fry)	300 ml

Preparation

- ❖ Peel wash and cut the onions into 2 mm thin slices.
- ❖ Soak the onion ring into buttermilk at least for 2 hours in advance (to get the more strong flavour).
- ❖ Squeeze the additional butter milk and coat with seasoned flour (refined flour mix salt, pepper, oregano and basil leaves.

Cooking Method

- ❖ Heat the oil at smoking points, deep fry the onion rings and remove from the oil.
- ❖ Sprinkle salt, powdered sugar and cayenne pepper.

Fajitas Veggies

The combination of veggies is used as base for fajita's hot set up.

Ingredients	Quantity
Mushrooms	100 gm
Tomato	30 gm
Capsicum green	30 gm
Capsicum red	30 gm
Onion	60 gm
Zucchini	50 gm
Margarine/oil	25 ml
Lime juice	1 no.
Water(if required)	15 ml
Salt	To taste
Cayenne pepper	3 gm
White pepper	2 gm
Vinegar	10 ml
Thyme	3 gm
Oregano	2 gm

Preparation

- Wash all the vegetables and slice mushroom in thin slices.
- Deseed tomato and capsicum and shred.
- Slice onion and zucchini into thin strips and coarsely chop the mushrooms.

Method

- Over high heat, put oil and sauté onion for about 2-3 minutes and add zucchini.
- Let cook for about 3-5 minutes, adding water if needed so it won't stick.
- Add the mushrooms, capsicum and lime juice and sauté for just about 1-2 minutes.
- Add seasonings and mix well.

Fajita Seasoning Mix

Ingredients	Quantity
Cornstarch	45 gm
Chili powder	30 gm
Salt	15 gm
Paprika	15 gm
Sugar	15 gm
Onion powder	20 gm
Garlic powder	2.5 gm
Cayenne pepper	2.5 gm
Crushed red pepper flakes	1 gm
Cumin	2.5 gm

PREPARATION

- ❖ Combine all of the ingredients in a small bowl.
- ❖ Grind tem in to fine powder.
- ❖ Strain through fine strainer.
- ❖ Put into airtight container, seal tightly, and store in a cool, dry place.

Vegetable Stock

This is basic preparation which generally we use in the making of various soups, rice and other preparations to get more prominent flavour.

Ingredient	Quantity
Olive oil	20 ml
Onion	30 gm
Celery stalk with some leaves	20 gm
Carrot	30 gm
Garlic	15 gm
Parsley	10 gm
Water	750 ml
Bay leaves	02 nos
Mushroom	4-5 nos
Whole black pepper	8-10 nos

Preparation

- ❖ Wash, peel and roughly chop vegetables.
- ❖ Heat oil in a soup pot. Add onion, celery, carrots, scallions, garlic, parsley, thyme, and bay leaves.
- ❖ Cook over high heat for few minutes, stirring frequently.
- ❖ Add salt and water and bring to a boil.
- ❖ Lower heat and simmer, uncovered, for 15-20 minutes. Strain. Discard vegetables.
- ❖ Stock is ready for use.

Chicken Stock

This is basic preparation which generally we use in the making of various soups,rice and other preparations to get more prominent flavour.

Ingredient	Quantity
Chicken Bones	400gm
Olive oil	20 ml
Onion	30 gm
Celery stalk with some leaves	20 gm
Carrot	30 gm
Garlic	15 gm
Parsley	10 gm
Bay leaves	02 nos
Mushroom	4-5 nos
Whole black pepper	8-10 nos

Preparation

- Clean and wash chicken bones.
- Wash, peel and roughly chop vegetables.
- Heat oil in a soup pot. Add onion, celery, carrots, garlic, parsley, thyme, and bay leaves.
- Cook over high heat for few minutes, stirring frequently.
- Add salt and water and bring to a boil.
- Lower heat and simmer, uncovered, for 25-30 minutes.
- Sieve the stock carefully with the help of strainer and remove bones, whole spices and vegetables from it.
- Stock is ready for instant use or it may store for further use after its cooling.

Mayonnaise Sauce

Mayonnaise can significantly enhance the flavor of a variety of different salads, sandwiches and appetizers.

Ingredients	Quantity
Eggs yolk (at room temperature)	03 nos
Lemon juice	10 ml
Olive oil	375 ml
Salt	To taste
White pepper	A pinch
Superfine sugar	5 gm
Mustard powder	3 gm

Preparation

- ❖ Weigh and place all ingredients together.
- ❖ Separate the egg yolk from whites and place the egg yolks in a small bowl.
- ❖ Pour the fresh lemon juice, mustard powder, superfine sugar into the bowl with the egg yolks and whisk them well.
- ❖ Slowly, a few drops at a time, pour the oil into the bowl while whisking constantly. Once the mayonnaise has started to thicken, pour the oil in a slow and steady stream.
- ❖ Once all the oil has been mixed well, correct the seasoning.
- ❖ Store mayonnaise in the refrigerator in a covered container for 2-3 days.

Mexican Potato Salad

Ingredients	Quantity
Red Potatoes, cut into chunks	450 gm
Corn kernels, thawed	120 gm
Tomato, chopped	100 gm
Scallions*, chopped	15 gm
Mayonnaise Sauce	75 ml
Chopped green chillies	3 nos
Fresh lime juice	40 ml
Fresh cilantro leaves chopped	10 gm
Freshly ground pepper	3 gm

* *Scallion is a kind of green onion but have a milder taste than most onions.*

** *Mayonnaise Sauce.*

Preparation

- ❖ Place the potatoes in a large pot and cover with water.
- ❖ Bring to a boil, reduce the heat, cover, and cook 30 minutes, or until just tender.
- ❖ Remove from the heat, drain, and place in large bowl and cut the red potatoes into dices of ½ inch.
- ❖ Thaw the corn kernels fresh one, otherwise blanch it in hot water for few minutes.
- ❖ Clean, wash and finely chopped tomato and scallions.

ASSEMBLING

- ❖ Add the corn, green chillies and scallions.
- ❖ Combine mayonnaise and lime juice.
- ❖ Pour over the salad and mix well. Add seasoning.
- ❖ Add the fine chopped coriander leaves.
- ❖ Mix gently and serve chill.

Black Bean and Corn Salad

Ingredients	Quantity
Black beans	120 gm
Corn kernel	12 0gm
Lemon juice	20 ml
Chopped Jalapenos	4 nos
Onion	60 gm
Celery	15 gm
Chopped Coriander leaves	5 gm
Salt	To taste
White pepper	A pinch

Preparation

- Clean, wash and soak black beans for at least 6 hours.
- Refresh with fresh water. Boil in salted water until the beans get enough tender.
- Remove the stem and seed from the red pepper and cut into ½ inche cube.
- Remove the stem and see from the jalapenos and chopped finely.
- Peel the onion and chopped finely.
- Combine the sour cream and mayonnaise sauce until mix blended.
- Mix the beans, corn and other ingredients.
- Toss well & store in a covered bowl in the refrigerator for few hours and served chilled.

Tomato & Tortilla Soup

Ingredients	Quantity
Onions	120 gm
Cloves garlic	10 gm
Green chillies	30 nos
Vegetable oil	40 ml
Cumin powder	3 gm
Oregano	2 gm
Fresh tomatoes	75 gm
Vegetable stock	600 ml
lime juice	20 ml
Tortilla chips, crushed	45 gm
Chopped fresh cilantro leaves	10 gm
Salt	To taste

Preparation

- Peel and finely chopped onion.
- Press, crush and garlic.
- Clean, wash and finely chopped tomatoes and cilantro leaves.

Cooking Method

- In medium pan & sauté onions and garlic in oil.
- Add chillies, cumin, oregano and sauté a few minutes.
- Add tomatoes.
- Sprinkle tomatoes with salt.
- Cover gently until tomatoes begin to release juices.
- Stir occasionally.
- Add stock and simmer, covered, for 15 minutes.
- Add lime juice and salt to taste.
- Topped with tortilla chips, garnish with cilantro leaves and serve hot.

Mexican Onion Soup

Ingredients	Quantity
Yellow onion	350gm
Garlic	10 nos
Butter	30gm
Tomato juice	240 ml
Stock	120 ml
Tomato salsa	60 ml
Salt & pepper	To taste
Grated cheese	100 gm

Preparation

- Remove the skin from the onion and slice into rings. Remove the skin from the garlic clove and mince.
- Grate cheese.

Method

- Melt the butter over medium heat in a large frying pan. Add the onion and cook for few minutes, stir frequently. Onion should be tender the light brown.
- Stir the tomato juice, stock and salsa. Bring to boil and reduce the flame.
- Simmer for approx 15 me minutes. Top with grated cheese before serving.

Vegetable Tortilla Soup

Ingredients	Quantity
Corn Tortilla	80 gm
Carrot	100gm
Onion	100gm
Garlic	5 nos
Red Capsicum	50 gm
Frozen Corn	150 gm
Tomato	200 gm
Butter	30 gm
Stock	120 ml
Cayenne Pepper	3 gm
Cumin Powdered	10 gm
Stock	300 ml
Lime Juice	30 ml
Coriander Leaves	5 gm
Refined oil	300 ml
Salt & pepper	To taste

Preparation

- Take tortilla and cut into small dices of ½ inches and deep fried and keep aside.
- Peel the carrot and get the brunnoise.
- Peel the onion and get the brunnoise
- Peel the garlic, crush and chopped finely. .

- Peel and remove the shell of green peas.
- Wash and get shred the spinach.
- Wash, peel and cut the potatoes into small dices.
- Cut the capsicum into slices.
- Thaw the frozen corn.
- Chop the tomatoes into 1 inch cube.

Cooking Method

- Heat the stockpot and add butter.
- Sauté onion, garlic, carrot and stir for few minutes.
- Add all the vegetables one by one, stir well. Add stock.
- Cook for 20-25 minutes.
- Correct the seasoning.
- Garnish with chopped coriander leaves and serve hot crispy fried corn tortillas.

Mexican Black Bean Soup

Ingredients	Quantity
Black bean	60 gm
Vegetable stock*	600 ml
carrot	40gm
Ginger	10 gm
Onion	60gm
Garlic	6 nos
Sugar	A pinch
Jalapenos	10 nos
Lemon juice	20 ml
Tomato puree	100 ml
Refined oil Butter	30 gm+ 20 ml
Fennel seed powder	5 gm
Dried basil leaves	2 gm
Cumin powdered	10 gm
Coriander leaves	5 gm
Cayenne pepper	A pinch
Salt & pepper	To taste

**follow the recipe of vegetable stock at page #*

Preparation

- ❖ Clean, wash and soak black beans overnight in sufficient water.
- ❖ Peel onion, ginger & garlic and chopped finely.
- ❖ Wash, peel and cut the carrot into small dices.

Cooking Method

- ❖ Heat the stockpot and add butter sauté onion, ginger, garlic, carrot and sauté for few minutes.
- ❖ Add black beans, tomato puree & vegetable stock bring to boil, then lower the temperature. Simmer the soup until the beans are soft.
- ❖ Now add fennel seed powder, roasted cumin powder, basil, salt and cayenne pepper and black pepper.
- ❖ Add lime juice at the last, garnish with chopped coriander leaves and serve hot.

Creamy Corn Soup

Ingredients	Quantity
Onion	80 gm
Tomato	120 gm
Frozen corn	350 gm
Vegetable Stock	450 ml
Freshly ground pepper	4 gm
Salt	To taste
Whipped cream	100 ml

Preparation

- Peel the onion and cut into quarter.
- Remove the skin of the tomato and cut into quarters.
- Put the corn, tomatoes and 100 ml stock in a food processor and process to get the grainy texture.

Cooking Method

- Take a stock pot and place the prepared mixture along with remaining stock on medium flame.
- Add the seasoning. Heat thoroughly but don't boil.
- Stir in the whipped cream and cook on low heat and serve piping hot.

Soup

Chicken Tortilla Soup

Ingredients	Quantity
Chopped Chicken	100 gm
Fried corn tortilla	4 nos
Onion	80 gm
Garlic	10 gm
Red bell pepper	40 gm
Tomato	60 gm
Cayenne pepper	4 gm
Roasted ground cumin	5 gm
Crushed black pepper	3 gm
Sugar	5 gm
Chicken stock *	750 ml
Frozen corn	350 gm
Lime juice	30 ml
Refined oil	25 mi
Salt	To taste
Whipped cream	100 ml
Refined oil for frying tortillas	

**Recipe of chicken stock*

Preparation

- Clean, wash and cut chicken in the dices of 10 cm.
- Wash & peel the onion and garlic & chop it finely.

- Deseed the tomatoes, remove the stem of red bell pepper and cut into small dices.
- Remove frozen corn from deep freezer and refresh with fresh water.

Cooking Method

- Deep fry corn tortilla in hot fat, remove from hot fat and keep a side.
- Take a stock pot add oil and make hot enough add chopped garlic, sauté it for some time.
- Add onion and again sauté for few seconds.
- Now add red bell pepper, corn and chicken dices and cook for some times.
- Add chicken stock, bring a boil, and reduce the flame cook until chicken get tender.
- Add cayenne pepper, cumin powder, sugar, salt & Mix well.
- Remove soup from the fire, pour soup individual soup cups add lime juice, crushed tortilla in it, garnish with chopped coriander leaves, topped with whipped cream at last & serve hot.

Potato Tacos

Ingredients	Quantity
Taco shell	04 nos
Potatoes	120 gm
Chopped green onions	2 nos
Cheddar cheese	45 gm
Sour Cream	60 ml
Tomato Salsa	45 ml
Taco seasoning	4 gm

Preparation

- Wash, peel and chopped potatoes.
- Wash, peel and chopped green onion.
- Grate cheese.

Method

- Boil potatoes in salted water.
- Drain remaining water from the potatoes and transfer to a bowl.
- Cut the potatoes in 5 cm cubes.
- Add onions, cheese and salsa, taco seasoning, jalapenos and mix well.
- Put the prepared mixture into the center of each taco shell.
- Arrange taco shells in a serving platter.
- Serve with sour cream and tomato salsa.

Chicken Tacos

Ingredients	Quantity
Taco shells	04 nos
Chicken breast	300 gm
Zucchini (roughly chopped)	40 gm
Onion, chopped	50 gm
Garlic clove, chopped	10 gm
Tomato, chopped	30 gm
Cheddar cheese	60 gm
Corn tortillas	06 nos
Fresh mild green chilli	3 nos
Chopped jalapenos	2 nos
White pepper	4 gm
Olive oil	20 ml
Taco seasoning	5 gm
Ground cumin	A pinch
Oregano	A pinch
Fresh coriander chopped	A few sprigs
Refined oil (for frying)	

Preparation

- Clean, wash and marinate chicken breast with olive oil, salt, cayenne pepper and oregano.

Cooking Method

- Take a heavy skillet, add olive oil and grill the chicken breast from both the sides.

- ❖ Remove from the fire and finely shred the chicken.
- ❖ Heat a tablespoon or two of oil in a large sauté pan on medium high heat. Add the zucchini, onions, garlic, green chillies and jalapeño to the pan.
- ❖ Sprinkle with salt and cumin. Stir to coat the vegetables with the oil in the pan.
- ❖ Stir the veggies occasionally, until they become lightly browned.
- ❖ Stir in the chopped tomatoes and oregano, lower the heat to low.
- ❖ Heat a pan, add olive oil, and add fine chop onion, garlic & green chillies.
- ❖ Sauté for a while, add tomatoes, chopped jalapeño & mix well. Add taco seasoning and other powdered spices.
- ❖ Fill the mixture of veggies in tacos cell, cover with cheese, bake in pre heated oven to get cheese brown.
- ❖ Remove from oven, garnish with chopped cilantro leaves, jalapenos and served with sour cream and roasted garlic salsa.

Veggie Tacos

Ingredients	Quantity
Taco shells	04 nos
Olive oil	30 ml
zucchini (roughly chopped)	90 gm
onion, chopped	60 gm
garlic clove, chopped	10 gm
tomato, chopped	30 gm
Green chillies	03 nos
cheddar cheese	60 gm
fresh mild green chilli	30 nos
Chopped jalapenos	2 nos
White pepper	4 gm
Salt	To taste
Ground cumin	A pinch
Oregano dry	A pinch
Fresh coriander leaves chopped	A few sprigs

METHOD

- Heat a tablespoon or two of oil in a large sauté pan on medium high heat. Add the zucchini, onions, garlic, green chillies and jalapeño to the pan.
- Sprinkle with salt and cumin. Stir to coat the vegetables with the oil in the pan.
- Spread the veggies out in the pan and then stir only occasionally, until they are all lightly browned.

- Stir in the chopped tomatoes and oregano.
- Heat a pan, add olive oil, and add fine chop onion, garlic & green chillies. Sauté for a while, add tomatoes, chopped jalapeño & mix well. Add taco seasoning and mix well.
- Fill this mixture in tacos cell, cover with cheese and bake in pre heated oven to get cheese brown.
- Remove from the oven, arrange in a platter, garnish with chopped cilantro leaves, jalapenos and served with sour cream and roasted garlic salsa.

Vegetable Roll

Ingredients	Quantity
Flour tortilla 8"	4 nos
Jalapenos	5-6 nos
Onion	60 gm
Green Capsicum	60 gm
Yellow pepper	50
Red bell pepper	50
Tomato	60 gm
Olive oil	45 ml
Cheese	240 ml
Garlic powder	A pinch
Cayenne pepper	A pinch
Salt	To taste
Red chilli flakes	1 gm
White Pepper	A pinch
Salsa	60 ml
Sour cream	50 gm

METHOD

- ❖ Remove the stem and seed from the chilli and chopped finely.
- ❖ Remove the roots from the green onion and sliced finely.
- ❖ Wash, cut sides of capsicum and cut it into fine slices.
- ❖ Wash and cut tomatoes into quarters first, deseed and cut it into fine slices.

- Grate cheese.
- Mix all ingredients.
- Take one tortilla and put approximately 60-70 gm of filling, spread the prepared mixture on tortillas and make a roll.
- Heat griddle plate or pan, drizzle little olive oil and bake it from both the side till it get light golden brown colour.
- Remove from pan, cut it a presentable way and serve with salsa and sour cream.

Cheese Quesadillas

Ingredients	Quantity
Flour tortillas 9"	04 nos
Grated cheese	240 ml
Olive oil	30 ml
Salt	to taste
Ranchero sauce	80 ml
Red chili powder	3 gm
Jalapenos	15 gm
Diced tomatoes	60 gm
Ice burg lettuce	30 gm
Chopped cilantro leaves	Few springs
Sour cream	30 ml
Tomato salsa	45 ml

Preparation

- ❖ Wash all the vegetables, deseed tomato & cut into lengthwise.
- ❖ Deseed capsicum and shred finely.
- ❖ Finely shred lettuce leaves (ice burg).
- ❖ Cut jalapenos in thin slices.
- ❖ Finely chopped coriander leaves.
- ❖ Cooking Method:
- ❖ Heat a heavy pan (non stick if possible), apply very little oil).
- ❖ Put one flour tortilla and apply sauce on the complete tortilla.

- ❖ Divide all the ingredients into four portions to fill each tortilla.
- ❖ Sprinkle grated cheese on half of the tortilla; add dices tomatoes red chilli powder, jalapenos and salt.
- ❖ Cover with remaining half part of tortilla.
- ❖ Bake from both the side in its light golden brown colour.
- ❖ Remove from heat. Cut into four pieces.
- ❖ Serve with salsa, sour cream, shredded ice burg & diced tomatoes.

Chicken Quesadillas

Ingredients	Quantity
Flour tortillas (9" inches)	4 nos
Grilled chicken breast	240 gm
Grated cheese	220 gm
Sliced green onions	40gm
Ground cumin	2 gm
Cayenne pepper powder	3 gm
Butter, melted	30 gm
Salt	to taste
Dried oregano leaves	2 gm
Lime juice	20 ml
Fruity Salsa	75 ml
Sour cream	100 ml

Preparation

- ❖ Clean, wash and boil chicken breast in salted water.
- ❖ Grate cheese.
- ❖ Wash, peel and sliced green onion.

Method

- ❖ Take a fry pan, and melt butter.
- ❖ Add sliced onion and sauté for few minutes.
- ❖ Add slices of cooked chicken breast; add cumin powder, salt oregano and cayenne pepper powder.
- ❖ Add lime juice, mix well and remove the mixture from fire.

- Keep aside.
- Brush one side of flour tortilla with butter; place buttered side down on a lightly greased baking sheet.
- Spread one fourth mixture over half of each tortilla; sprinkle with one fourth quantity of cheeses on half portion of each tortilla.
- Cover it with remaining portion of tortillas.
- Bake it in pre heated oven at 375°C for 10 minutes or until become crisp and golden brown.
- Cut into wedges; serve with sour cream and fruity salsa.

Corn Tortilla with Fresh Tomato Salsa

Ingredients	Quantity
Fried Corn Tortilla	20-22 nos
Fresh tomato Salsa	60 ml
Sour cream	30 ml
Refined oil for frying	

How to Serve

- Take 6′ corn tortilla, cut into four quarters and remove its round poertion in order to get the triangle shape.
- Heat refined oil in a frying pan. Deep fry corn tortilla.
- Fry till it become light golden brown in colour and gets crispy in texture.
- Now, take a platter and arrange tortillas in it and serve with fresh tomato salsa and sour cream.

Super Nachos

Ingredients	Quantity
Corn Tortilla	15-20 pieces
Red Chilli Beans	90 ml
Chopped Jalapenos	4-6 nos
Diced tomatoes	60 gm
Cheddar cheese, shredded	120 gm
Diced Tomato	100 gm
For serving	
Tomato Salsa	60 ml
Sour cream	30 ml

Cooking Method

- Take a platter and arrange half of the tortillas in single layer.
- Pour red kidney beans on each tortilla.
- Grate cheese on the beans and put it in an oven till the cheese gets light golden brown in colour.
- Remove from the oven and sprinkle diced tomatoes and jalapenos on it.
- Repeat the process by using the remaining half of the tortilla, red kidney beans and cheese.
- Remove from oven, add diced tomatoes and jalapenos.
- Remove from the oven and serve with sour cream and tomato salsa.

Corn tortilla with Peri Peri sauce

Ingredients	Quantity
Corn tortilla (2 inch round)	10-12 nos
Peri peri sauce	20ml
Sour cream	30 ml

HOW TO SERVE

❖ Take a platter, arrange round corn tortillas and serve with periperi sauce and sour cream.

Olive & Herb Tortilla with Peri Peri Sauce

Ingredients	Quantity
Olive and herb tortilla (2 inch round)	10-12 nos
Peri peri sauce	20ml
Sour cream	30 ml

How to serve

❖ Take a platter, arrange round corn tortillas and serve with periperi sauce and sour cream.

Vegetable Chimichanga

Ingredients	Quantity
Garlic cloves, minced	4Nos
Olive oil	15 ml
Arabiata sauce	220 ml
Salt	To taste
Powdered cumin	2 gm
Sour cream	60ml
Grated cheddar cheese	50 ml
Egg wash	01 no
Oil for frying	400 ml
For Filling	
Flour tortillas 12 "	4 nos
Shredded carrot	60 gm
Shredded bottle gourd	60 gm
Shredded capsicum	60 gm
Jalapenos	10 nos
Salt	60
Cheese	180 gm
Accompaniment	
Rice pilaf *	240 gm
Red chilli beans	80 ml

* *follow the recipe of rice pilaf.*

PREPARATION FOR FILLING

- Shred the carrot, capsicum, gourd with the thickness of slice of 3 mm width.
- Squeeze out the water from these shredded vegetables as moisture will lead to the tearing of the tortilla while wrapping.
- Drain out the brine solution from the chillies. Then finely chop the chillies.
- Mix all the ingredients in a mixing bowl. Add grated cheese and divide the filling into four equal portions.
- Take one tortilla, put one part of filling at the upper side apply egg wash on outer side.
- Fold from the outside toward centre and then fold in cylindrical form.
- Prepare rest pieces in the same way.
- Wrap the Chimichanga with cling warp for at least 15 minutes so that they become set from sides.
- Remove from sheet, heat the oil and deep fry the Chimichanga till golden brown in colour.
- Remove from oil.
- Take a baking dish and arrange two Chimichanga rolls and pour Arabiata sauce on each piece. Cover with grated cheese and bake in pre heated oven for few minutes.
- How to assemble:
- Take two pieces of Chimichanga, rice pilaf topped with red chilli beans along with sour cream, diced tomato and tomato salsa.

Chicken Chimichanga

Ingredients	Quantity
Flour Tortilla 9"	04 nos
Boneless Chicken	350 gm
Onion, chopped	50 gm
Garlic	15 gm
Refined oil	30 ml
Salt	To taste
Cayenne Pepper	3 gm
Ranchero Sauce	200 ml
Refined oil for frying	
Egg	01 no
For Serving	
Salsa	60 ml
Cheddar cheese, shredded	120 gm
Red Chilli Beans	90 ml
Shredded Ice burg	20 gm
Diced Tomato	10 gm
Rice Pilaf	100 gm
Sour cream	20 ml

PREPARATIONS

- Preheat oven at 250 °C.
- Mince chicken.
- Chop onion and garlic.

- Wash, cut into quarter, deseed and then cut into small dices of tomato.
- Shred iceberg.

Cooking Method

- Take a saucepan, add refined oil. Add chopped onion and garlic. Sauté for few minutes.
- Add mince chicken and sauté it. Add half of the quantity of ranchero sauce, jalapenos and seasoning. Cook till the chicken become tender.
- Remove from flame, allow the mixture cool.
- Now, add grated cheese and lime juice and mix well.
- Now take one piece of tortilla, spread 30 ml of ranchero sauce, 50 gm of the prepared filling one end of the tortilla. Make one roll, apply egg wash on the both open sides if the Chimichanga. Now, completely roll to the Chimichanga and at the end side, again apply egg wash to make seal properly.
- Prepare rest of the chimchamga's roll and keep it in refrigerator for at least 01 hour.
- Heat oil and deep fry Chimichanga till golden brown colour.
- Take two pieces of Chimichanga in a baking tray, pour ranchero sauce and grated cheese on the top.
- Bake it in pre heated oven for 4-5 minutes at 200°C.

How to serve

- Arrange two piece of Chimichanga in a serving plate along with rice pilaf topped with red kidney beans, shredded Iceburg topped with diced tomato, salsa and sour cream.

Vegetable Enchilada

Ingredients	Quantity
Flour tortillas 8"	4 nos
For Filling	
Red kidney beans (roughly paste)	150 gm
Butter	10 gm
Mix cheese *	4240 gm
Garlic chopped	10 gm
Onion chopped	10 gm
Salt	To taste
White pepper	1 gm
Garlic powder	1 gm
Red chilli flakes	2 gm
Refined oil	10 gm
Ranchero sauce**	120 ml
For assembling	
olive oil	15 ml
Head of garlic	10 gm
Jalapeños, diced	1no
Whole black olives, rinsed, drained and sliced-	5 gm
Grated Cheddar cheese (for topping)	60 gm

**Jack & Colby cheese in equal proportion*

Jack cheese	50 gm
Colby cheese	50 gm
Corn flour	2 gm

*** follow the recipe*

Cooking Method

- Wash and soak kidney beans for at least 6 hour
- Refresh with fresh water and cook it with salted water and cook till it become tender enough.
- Allow to cool, make fine paste of boiled kidney beans.
- Take pan, heat butter in a pan, sauté garlic & onion.
- Cook onion and garlic till they get brown.
- Add mix cheese & cook for a while.
- Add red chilli flakes.
- Pre-heat oven to 250°C.
- Heat olive oil in a skillet over low heat and add finally chopped garlic and onion.
- Add jalapeños and sauté for few seconds.
- Add enchilada filling and cook for few minutes and then add Mix cheese.
- Remove from heat and cheese well with the other ingredients.
- Take one flour tortilla and apply ranchero sauce on both sides of tortilla.
- Put enchilada filling, olives and cheese make a roll and make another portions in the same manner.
- Take two pieces of enchiladas and topped with grated cheese
- Place stuffed enchilada in the oven and bake for sometimes to get the cheese melt and gets light golden brown colour.

How to serve

- Arrange two pieces of enchiladas in a serving plate along with rice pilaf topped with red kidney beans, shredded Iceburg topped with diced tomato, salsa and sour cream.

Mexican Meatballs

Ingredients	Quantity
For meatballs	
Minced mutton	450 gm
Onion, finely chopped	100 gm
Fresh breadcrumbs, toasted	60 gm
Dried oregano	5 gm
Ground cumin	4 gm
Egg, beaten	01 no
Refined oil for frying	
For the sauce	
Jalapenos chilli, seeds removed	30 gm
Vegetable oil	30 ml
Onion, finely chopped	30 gm
Cloves garlic, finely chopped	15 gm
chicken stock*	100 ml
chopped tomatoes	150 gm
Cheese	20 gm

** Use the recipe of chicken stock.*

Cooking Method

- ❖ For the sauce: soak the chillies in a little warm water for 15 minutes.
- ❖ For Meatballs: Combine the onion, pork and beef in a mixing bowl. Add the breadcrumbs, oregano, cumin and ½ teaspoon each of salt and pepper and mix well.

- ❖ Add the egg and mix thoroughly. Roll the mixture into balls about 4cm in diameter.
- ❖ Heat the oil in a frying pan, add the meatballs and fry for 5-7 minutes, turning occasionally, until gets light brown in colour .
- ❖ Remove from oil and keep a side.
- ❖ Finely chop the chillies.
- ❖ Take a pan, combine oil, jalapenos, onion, garlic, stock, tomatoes and some salt and pepper. Bring to the boil and simmer for 5-7 minutes.
- ❖ Add the meatballs to the sauce and simmer for 10-15 minutes.
- ❖ Garnish with cheese.
- ❖ Serve it as it is or with rice pilaf, salsa and sour cream.

Cottage Cheese Fajita

Ingredients For fajita	Quantity
Cottage cheese	600 gm
To marinate cottage cheese	
Cayenne pepper	8 gm
Olive oil	30 ml
Lemon Juice	20 ml
Salt	to taste
Freshly ground white pepper	2 gm
Onion	120 gm
Red capsicum	100 gm
Green capsicum	100
For cold fajita set up	
Flour tortilla 6"	8 nos
Onion straws *	60 gm
Red kidney beans	90 gm
Sour cream	60 ml
Tomato salsa	60 ml
Shredded lettuce leaves	40 gm
Green coriander leaves	3 gm
Diced tomatoes	Gm
To fire fajitas	
Olive oil	10 ml
Lemon juice	10 ml
Butter	10 gm

Use onion straws recipe.

Preparation

- Cut cottage cheese into triangle with the thickness of 10 cm.
- Take a tossing bowl and use half of the quantity of all ingredients for marination and keep aside.
- Add all ingredients to marinate cottage cheese.
- Mix well and put the triangles of cottage cheese in the marination for at least 1 hour.
- Peels onion and wash other vegetables also.
- Cut half moon shape in 3 mm thickness to red and green capsicum.
- Cut tomatoes into quarters, deseed and cut into 5 mm dices.
- Finely shred to lettuce leaves and coriander leaves.

Cooking Method

- Put the fajita plate on fire and keep it on fire till become red hot.
- Take a heavy bottom pan, add butter and allow to melt.
- Add marinated cottage cheese slices and cook till it become light golden brown in colour.
- Sprinkle cayenne pepper and oregano on the top.
- Prepare Fajita cold setup in another plate which includes two pieces of flour tortilla, rice pilaf topped with red kidney beans, sour cream and tomato salsa.
- Sprinkle grated cheese on red kidney beans and fine chopped coriander leaves on sour cream.
- Keep shredded lettuce leaves topped with diced tomatoes, sour cream and salsa.

How to Serve Fajita

- Take a fry pan and melt butter. Add sliced onion & capsicum and sauté for few minutes.

- Add salt, pepper and cayenne pepper. Add lemon juice at last and mix well
- Transfer red hot fajita plate on wooden base.
- Place these sautéed vegetables. And placed grilled cottage cheese slices on these vegetables.
- Add last, fire fajita by pouring the mixture of olive oil and vinegar over the cottage cheese and put some butter on hot iron skillet to produce enough smoke while serving the fajitas.
- Serve fajita along with cold fajita set up.

Chicken Fajita

Ingredients	Quantity
For fajitas	
Chicken breast (80- 90 gm each)	350 gm
Olive oil	30 ml
Onion	120 gm
Red capsicum	100 gm
Green capsicum	100 gm
Cayenne pepper	10 gm
Butter	40 gm
Lemon juice	20 ml
Salt	to taste
Freshly ground white pepper	2 gm
For Cold Fajita set up	
Flour tortilla 6"	8 nos
Onion straws **	60 gm
Red kidney beans	150 gm
Sour cream	120 ml
Tomato salsa	120 ml
Shredded lettuce leaves	40 gm
Green coriander leaves	3gm
Diced tomatoes	30 ml
To fire fajitas	
Olive oil	10 ml
Lemon juice	10 ml
Butter	10 gm

**onion straws recipe.*

Preparation

- Wash chicken breast under running water after washing wipe with dry cloth.
- Prick the chicken breast with fork to absorb the marination inside properly.
- Take a stainless bowl and prepare Marination by using olive oil, salt pepper, cayenne pepper, oregano, lemon juice and mix well.
- Put the chicken breasts in the marination for at least 4 to 6 hours to get the strong flavour.
- Peels onion and wash other vegetables also.
- Cut half moon shape in 3 mm thickness to red and green capsicum.
- Cut tomatoes into quarters, deseed and cut into 5 mm dices.
- Finely shred to lettuce leaves and coriander leaves.

Cooking Method

- Put the fajita plate on fire and keep it on fire till become red hot.
- Take a heavy bottom pan, melt butter and put the marinated chicken breast and cook till it become tender enough and become light golden brown.
- Sprinkle cayenne pepper on both the sides.
- Season with salt and freshly white ground pepper and half of the quantity of cayenne pepper.
- Cut the chicken breast into length wise half inche thick slices and keep aside.
- Prepare fajita setup in another plate which includes two nos of flour tortilla, rice pilaf topped with red kidney beans, sour cream and tomato salsa for per person

- Sprinkle grated cheese on red kidney beans and fine chopped coriander leaves on sour cream.
- Keep shredded lettuce leaves topped with diced tomatoes. Except sour cream, salsa, shredded lettuce leaves and diced tomatoes, rest all the things serve hot in this setup.

How to serve Fajita

- Take a fry pan and melt butter.
- Add slices of onion, capsicum, mushroom and sauté for few minutes.
- Add salt, pepper and cayenne pepper.
- Transfer red hot fajita plate on wooden base loaded with sautéed vegetables.
- Places grilled cottage cheese slices on these vegetables.
- Add last, fire fajita by pouring the mixture of olive oil and vinegar over the grilled chicken and put some butter on hot iron skillet to produce enough smoke while serving the fajitas.
- Serve fajita along with cold fajita set up.

Mexican Rice

Ingredients	Quantity
Rice	200 gm
Green capsicum	25 gm
Yellow capsicum	20 gm
Red capsicum	20 gm
Jalapenos	8 nos
Garlic cloves	10 gm
Onion	80 gm
Olive Oil	30 ml
Vegetable Stock	300 gm
Coriander leaves	few spring

Preparation

- Wash and peel onion & garlic and finally chop it.
- Wash all types of peppers (green, yellow & red) & cut into small dice.
- Roughly chopped tomatoes. Boil tomatoes in water until skin bursts.

Cooking Method

- Take a heavy bottom stock pot.
- Add olive oil and add garlic, onion and all types of diced capsicum and sauté for few minutes.
- Add rice and again sauté for few minutes.
- Add vegetable stock, bring to boil and once it reaches at boiling stage, slow the flame and cover it with tightly fitted lid.

- Cook till rice gets tender.
- Remove from the fire, open the lid.
- Arrange rice in a platter, garnish with chopped coriander leaves and serve hot.

Jalapenos Rice

Ingredients	Quantity
Long grain rice	250gm
Refined oil	20 ml
Butter	30 gm
Chopped Onion	30 gm
Garlic	10 gm
Sour Cream *	60 ml
Jalapenos	4 nos
Green chillies	3 nos
Vegetable stock	450 ml
Salt	to taste
White pepper	to taste

** Follow the recipe.*

Preparation

- ❖ Clean, wash and soak rice for 30 minutes.
- ❖ Finely chopped onion, green chillies, garlic and jalapenos.

Cooking Method

- ❖ Preheat oven to 350°C.
- ❖ Bring boil the water along with salt and refined oil.
- ❖ Add rice and cook for 5 to 6 minutes.
- ❖ Heat a frying pan; add butter and sauté garlic, onion and both types of chillies for few seconds.
- ❖ Layer the rice with sour cream and bake for 20 minutes
- ❖ Remove from the oven and serve with fresh salsa sauce. This rice may serve with main courses as accompaniment.

Mexican Chicken Rice

Ingredients	Quantity
Boneless Chicken slices	120 gm
Long grain rice	200 gm
refined oil	20 ml
Milk	100 ml
Onion	30 ml
Garlic	10 gm
Butter	45 gm
Chicken stock	450 ml.
Cayenne pepper	3 gm
Salt	to taste
Nutmeg powder	4 gm
Taco seasoning	A pinch
Ground clove	4gm
Green Chillies	3 nos
Jalapenos	4 nos

Preparation

- Clean, wash and soak rice for 30 minutes.
- Finely chopped onion, garlic, green chilli and jalapenos.

Cooking Method

- Preheat oven to 250 °C.
- Bring boil the water along with salt and refined oil.

- ❖ Add rice and cook for 5 to 6 minutes.
- ❖ Heat a frying pan, add butter and sauté both types of chillies for few seconds.
- ❖ Layer the rice with sour cream and bake for 15- 20 minutes
- ❖ Remove from the oven and serve with fresh tomato salsa sauce.

Rice Pilaf

Ingredients	Quantity
Rice	200 gm
Vegetable stock*	450 ml
White pepper powder	3 gm
Butter	30 gm
Red onion, diced	200 gm
Red bell pepper	100 gm
Green bell pepper	100 gm
Fresh garlic fine chopped	10 gm
Salt	To taste
White pepper	

** Quantity of stock or water also depends upon the quality of the rice as well.*

Preparation

- Clean, wash and soak for 30 minutes.

Method

- Wash and rice for at least 30 min
- Heat butter in a stock pot.
- Sauté garlic along with onion & bell pepper.
- Add water & bring to boil.
- Add salt and pepper
- Add soaked rice to the water& cook till water is properly absorbed in the rice.

- Cover with butter paper or silver foil and place on hot plate for 5 to 7 minutes.
- Remove it from fire & allow to cool well.

Mexican Rice Pudding

Mexican Rice Pudding is a dish made from rice mixed with water or milk and other ingredients such as cinnamon and raisins.

Ingredients	Quantity
Uncooked long-grain white rice	50 gm
Water	50 ml
Milk	550 ml
Sugar	100 gm
Vanilla essence	Few drop
Cinnamon powder	03 gm
Raisins	15 gm

Cooking Method

- ❖ In a saucepan, combine water, rice and cinnamon sticks and bring to a boil. Reduce heat to simmer, cover pot and heat for 10 minutes or until water is absorbed.
- ❖ Add boiled milk, cover and continue to cook over low heat for another 20 minutes.
- ❖ Add the sugar and vanilla and continue to simmer (uncovered) for 3-5 minutes to dissolve sugar completely.
- ❖ Place into a large serving dish.
- ❖ Place cinnamon sticks on top, add raisins and sprinkle with ground cinnamon for garnish if desired. Serve warm or cold as a dessert.

Bionico

Bionico is a popular Mexican dessert, is essentially a fruit salad consisting of a variety of fruits chopped up into small dices, drenched with cream and honey.

Ingredients	Quantity
Apple	50 gm
Cantalope	50 gm
Mango	50 gm
Banana	001
Kiwi	01 no
Plum	2 nos
Shredded coconut	20 gm
For Dressing	
Sweetened condensed milk	50 gm
Sour cream	40 ml
Honey	30 ml
Cinnamon powder	5 gm

Preparation

- Wash all fruits properly.
- Peel off apple, Cantalope, banana and plum remove seeds and cut into small dices. Peel off kiwi and cut into small dices.
- Break to coconut shell, wash it , shred it and keep aside.

How to combine

- In a bowl combine sweetened condensed milk, Sour cream, honey and cinnamon mix together.
- Cut fruit up and place in bowl & top with the cream mixture. Then sprinkle with cinnamon powder and coconut on top.

Capirotada

Capirotada is a traditional Mexican food similar to a bread pudding.

Ingredients	Quantity
White bread	01 pkt
Salted butter	40 gm
Raisins	90 gm
Pineapple chunks, drained	100 gm
Chopped walnuts	100 gm
Colby cheese	100 gm
Egg	01 no
Cinnamon sticks	8 nos
Sugar	220 gm
Milk	220 gm

Cooking Method:

- Preheat oven at 180°C).
- Combine water, cinnamon, and sugar in a saucepan. Bring to a boil and let simmer for about 10- 15 minutes. Keep aside.
- Toast bread and butter each slice on one side. Arrange toast in a single layer in a large casserole dish.
- Sprinkle bread with raisins, nuts, and pineapple. Slice cheese and place over this mixture.
- Repeat layers until all bread is used, making sure enough cheese is left over for the top.
- Pour the cinnamon syrup mixture over everything in baking dish.
- Bake for 30 minutes. Remove from oven and cool for at least 15 minutes.

Cocadas

Cocadas are a traditional coconut cookies and they are particularly popular in Mexico and other countries too.

Ingredients	Quantity
Shredded sweetened coconut	450 gm
Sweetened condensed milk	120 gm
Cornstarch	45 gm
Almond essence	Few drops
Vanilla extract	Few drops
Sugar	60 gm
Confectioners' sugar (optional)	30 gm

Cooking Method

- Preheat oven to 190 °C.
- In a medium mixing bowl, stir together coconut, cornstarch, sugar condensed milk, almond extract, and vanilla extract. Let mixture sit for 3 to 5 minutes.
- Make balls of the prepared mixture of 20 gm weight approximately.
- Bake for 15 to 20 minutes until lightly golden brown.
- Remove from oven and cool on wire rack.
- Using fine meshed sieve, dust with confectioners' sugar.
- Cocadas is ready to serve.

Churros

Ingredients	Quantity
Butter	60 gm
Water	120 ml
Beaten egg	3 nos
Salt	A pinch
Refined flour	120 gm
Regular sugar	80 gm
Vegetable oil, for frying	
Cinnamon powder, optional	A pinch
Icing sugar	15 gm

Cooking Method

- In a small saucepan over medium heat, combine water, 2½ tablespoons sugar, salt and 2 tablespoons vegetable oil.
- Bring to a boil and remove from heat. Stir in flour until mixture forms a ball.
- Heat oil for frying in deep-fryer. Pipe strips of dough into hot oil using a pastry bag. Fry until golden; drain on paper towels.
- Prepare sugar syrup by combining sugar and water.
- Immerse fried churros in the sugar syrup. Remove immediately.
- Drizzle with cinnamon powder and icing sugar.

Mexican Cheese Cake

Ingredients	Quantity
Cream cheese	450 gm
Sour cream	15 ml
Salt	to taste
White pepper	a pinch
Chopped green chilies	10 gm
lightly beaten egg yolk	03 nos
Shredded cheddar cheese	320 gm
Chunky tomato salsa	120 ml
Tortilla chips or fresh vegetables	

Cooking Method

- ❖ In a large bowl, beat cream cheese, ½ cup sour cream and seasoning until smooth.
- ❖ Add eggs; beat on low speed just until combined. Stir in cheddar cheese and chilies.
- ❖ Transfer to a greased 9-in. spring form pan. Place on a baking sheet. Bake at 250°C for 25-30 minutes or until center is almost set.
- ❖ Cool on a wire rack for 10 minutes. Carefully run a knife around edge of pan to loosen; cool 1 hour longer.
- ❖ Refrigerate overnight. Just before serving, spread salsa over cheesecake.
- ❖ Serve with tortilla chips or vegetables.